Growing & Caring for
Natural Black Hair 101

Growing & Caring for Natural Black Hair 101

AND SKIN CARE TIPS

J Yvonne Jones

PO Box 250274
Milwaukee, WI 53225

Contact@sisthanatural.com

Printed in the United States of America

ISBN-13: 9780997091007
ISBN-10: 0997091002
Library of Congress Control Number: 2015960665
Caring 4 Natural Black Hair, Milwaukeew, WI

Table of Contents

Acknowledgement

would like to thank God for His Grace and Mercy and for always protecting and providing for me. I would like to thank Tyheshia for her advice on natural oil use and encouraging me to do more research on it. I want to thank Ms. Brenda for helping with editing. I would like to thank my friends for their prayers especially Ms. Yvonne.

I would like to thank my family for their support specifically my darling children Maurice & Shawn and my mother, Olga. I would be remiss if I did not give a shout-out to my sister-in-law Trina who is always looking out for me & my hair when I am in Toronto, which was the beginning of my natural hair journey.

Above all, I thank you for choosing this book so I can share my hair journey with you. I am very grateful.

Be Blessed.
JYJ

Introduction

Growing up in Jamaica I can remember my grandmother brushing out my hair and styling it into several braids. When I was old enough to start doing my own hair I did not like doing it at all. It was thick, and it took a long time for the comb to go through it. I hated washday, so needless to say I often would wash my hair once a month or less. And so most of the time I would wear scarfs or pull it into a ponytail.

Then in my teens I was allowed to get a relaxer. On that day heaven opened its gate and I heard the sound of music, "Haaha!!" My comb glided through the silky smooth strands on my head. Thereafter I went through many years of chemically relaxed hair. Over several years I began to see changes in my hair texture. Sometimes I would find chemical burn spots on my scalp. These spots look like sores that was healed and then turned black. My hair also began thinning out, "The horror!"

For many years black hair care consisted of some form of chemical treatment, weaves and/or hair extensions. Along the way we developed many universal hair routine such as; "If you are going on vacation and water is involved, e.g. water park; the beach, etc. then we must get our hair braided. If we are having a bad hair day then we put a wig or a hat on, Well!!"

Most of us choose to relax our hair over press N curl because sweat or water is our enemy. "We're melting!" Sometime in 2005 a natural hair revolution started and many women of color joined in. The curly girl method became an international hit for women of all races. I reluctantly stopped using relaxers in 2008 and began flat ironing after washes.

In 2012 I went to Toronto for my annual family visit, and in the past my sister in-law would set up a hair appointment for me. So that year I told her I wanted to try the curly girl method and she set me up with one of Toronto's best. The salon she took me to specialized in curly girl styles, but sadly they found it very difficult for my hair to maintain any curls. They suggested I cut my hair because I had flat iron damage; of course I said **"NO!!!"**

I came back to the States with an attitude of "whew! I'm not going to cut my hair." But deep down I really liked the curly look. So one day I got up and decided, "I'm going to do it." I knew better than to cut it myself so on May 2nd 2013 I went to a hair salon and did what I call phase 3 transition "The Big Chop."

My personal hair journey has allowed me to share with others my standard routine for hair and skin care 101 and I hope it will help you on your journey as well. So here goes!

Transitioning – "The big chop"

To transition is to cut off your chemically straightened hair and accept your natural curly or kinky strand. There are several steps to this phase and you may or may not go through all of them.

Phase One
"From relaxed hair to flat ironing only." I stayed in this phase for six years. I did not want to leave because it was the closest I could get my hair to looking like it was relaxed.

Phase Two
"Put the flat iron down and let the hair grow out without altering the texture of your natural strand." During this phase you may need to trim the ends of your hair because of flat iron damage. As the hair grows out protective styling is a great way to transition and hide damaged ends.

Phase Three
"To chop or not to chop that is the question?" Before you make the decision to chop, pull your hair back in a slick-down pony to get an idea of how your face will look with no hair. Once you chop there is no turning back.   Also be prepared for the reactions from friends and family. "Like it? Not like it?" But be strong and rock your chop!

Tip: *To prevent breakage due to dryness and damage during transition, keep your hair hydrated. Moisture is your friend.*

Phase Four

"Hair Changing!" Each month in my transition I was faced with new discoveries as my hair grew out. When I did the big chop I was surprised by what I found. It was like pulling up the carpet in my home and finding I had beautiful hard wood floors underneath that just needed some tender care.

I use to spend hundreds of dollars getting my hair chemically altered. I was one of those young girls who were embarrassed because my hair did not look like the models on the shampoo commercials or in the magazines. Now, when I see my Sistas rocking their natural strand, my face lights up because our hair no longer embarrasses us. I am So! So! Proud of us. Rock on my Sistas!

TIP:

- *As my hair transitioned, I discovered some hats did not fit very well because of the short hair. It took a long time to get my hair into a ponytail even with the use of bobby pins. My go to look then was my wash & go and my Teeny Weeny Afro (TWA).*
- *Styling was different from season to season. The way I was able to wear my hair during the spring changed the next spring.*
- *And the biggest surprise of all was <u>shrinkage!</u> After wetting my hair it would be elongated because the water stretched it. But, when my hair dries it withdrew like a turtle in its shell. I have an 80% shrink pattern. Your curl pattern may not have much shrinkage or you may find you have an Afro or a kinky look. Whatever your look is just rock your tress and don't compare your hair to the next natural sister, be uniquely you.*

Styling Tools

Maintaining natural hair may require some unique tools and products. You may need to use a comb or a brush in your styling routine but the less manipulation to the hair after styling the better it is. This will help to eliminate excess stress and breakage to the hair. Tools you may need for your natural hair routine includes:

Use your fingers to rake, stretch or smooth hair as you detangle. The fingers are the most effective tools in the process. It allows you to immediately feel the knots so you can safety untangle without breakage while applying products to the hair. This is the method I use.

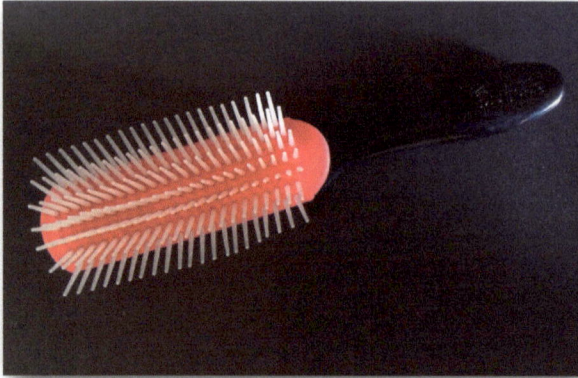

Using a brush with wide tooth will cause less damage to your hair.

If you must use a comb, a wide toothcomb would be preferred, best for all strands.

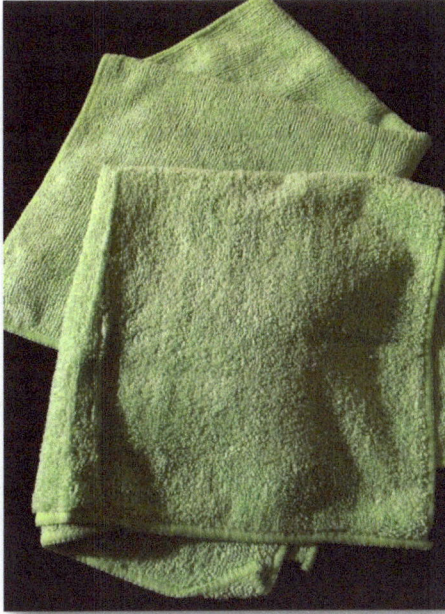

Use a microfiber towel (ultra absorbent) or an old t-shirt to dry your hair to eliminate frizzing. That's the 'angel hair glow' you get when your hair is dried with a regular towel. If you must use a towel, do not rub or move it around, pat dry to avoid frizzing and breakage of the hair.

Products

The use of natural products encourages hair to grow, naturally shines and reduces excessive hair loss. Treating your hair with a deep conditioner, hair mask, hot oil treatment, and shampoo will help to strengthen, and soften your hair. Steps for natural hair care products includes the following:

STEP ONE:

Pre-Wash or Pre-Poo
Using one of the following is an inexpensive do-it-yourself (DIY) method to cleanse your scalp from build-up of moisturizers, oils, gels and other products. Pre-poo eliminates the need to use harsh shampoos.

Option 1:

Apple Cider Vinegar Rinse

- One 8-ounce plastic spray bottle
- Two-tablespoons apple cider vinegar
- One cup of water, shake & on dry hair message into scalp

Option 2:

Baking Soda & Water Rinse

- Using an 8-ounce squeeze bottle, pour
- One tablespoon of baking soda-more based on thickness & length of hair
- Fill with water, shake to mix the baking soda and it's ready to use.
- Apply to hair in sections.

Tip: *If you have a favorite hair product that works then by all means use it, just check the ingredients to ensure it will not damage your efforts to grow out your hair.*

STEP TWO:

Shampoo

My routine consists of 80% co-washing and if product builds-up I would pre-poo before wash. Then with product in hand starting at the crown of the head, massage hair, concentrating on the scalp and move down to the ends of hair clarifying to remove build-up.

During this journey I tried to use products that were none toxic and did not strip my hair. So, if you must use a shampoo, try to find products with ingredients that have no harsh chemicals, to strip your hair of its moisture, color, or its natural oils. Avoid if you can, choosing products with alcohol, silicones or sulfate in the ingredients.

Option 1:

Co-Wash

Instead of using a regular shampoo to wash your hair use a conditioner. Conditioner is gentler on your hair and will not strip it of its natural oils and will still get the dirt out especially if you pre-wash. Saturate your hair with the conditioner and massage it into your scalp and hair. After you're finished rinse out with cool water.

Option 2:

DIY Herbal Wash - Heenara
This wash nourishes & conditions the hair leaving the hair soft & smooth.

- 3 - 4 tablespoons of Heenara into a glass bowl with cool water or Aloe Vera juice to make a paste
- Section hair and massage into scalp & leave in for 5 min.
- Rinse with warm or cool water.

STEP THREE:

Deep Conditioning
The process of deep conditioning will help to restore needed moisture to keep the hair healthy and soft. It will also provide protection from breakage while styling. After applying the conditioner, sit under a dryer for 20 minutes to allow the conditioner to penetrate deep into the shaft and cuticles.

Option 1:

DIY-Herbal Deep Conditioning

- 2 tablespoons of Shikakai powder
- 2 tablespoons of Neem powder
- 2 tablespoons of Alma powder
- 2 tablespoons of Aritha powder
- 2 tablespoons of Brahmi powder
- 5 drops of Amla oil
- 5 drops Shikakai oil
- 5 drops Bhringraj oil
- 5 drops of Black seed oil
- Or use your favorite carrier oil.

Blend into a paste by adding water or Aloe Vera juice. This combination is a super conditioner; it detangles, moisturize, thicken, cleanse, grow and darken the hair. Let mixture sit in your hair for 30 minutes to 1 hour. (Sometimes I keep it overnight) Cover your hair with a plastic cap to prevent the mixture from leaking or drying out. You may need to use an old tube sock, hand towel or scarf to keep the product from seeping down your head. Thoroughly rinse hair because the powder will feel sandy or grainy and will need extra time to wash out.

Tip: *DIY Herbal Deep conditioning products (Alma oil, Brahmi powder etc.) can be purchased on line or at most Indian grocery stores.*

Option 2:

Hot Oil Treatment

- 5 drops of Rosemary oil
- 5 drops of Lavender oil
- 2 tablespoons Coconut oil

Mix oils in small container then place container in warm water before applying to hair. Massage the scalp as you smooth the oil through the hair. Wrap with a warm towel and leave for 30 to 60 minutes before washing out.

Option 2:

Choose an alternate deep conditioner from the recommended products list at: www.sisthanatural.com

STEP FOUR:

Leave In Conditioning
Applying a leave-in after wash will moisturize, hydrate and soften the hair. When choosing a moisturizer the 1st ingredient should be water or aqua.

Section wet hair and apply healthy amounts of leave-in conditioner with your fingers, from ends to roots.

Tip: *When applying conditioner, work with small sections starting from the ends of the hair and work your way up to the roots.*

STEP FIVE:

DIY Oil Moisture
After applying your water base moisturizer to your hair apply a small amount of oil, about the size of a quarter depending on length of hair as the final step. Oils are used to create a barrier around the shaft, which will seal the strand to trap the water onto the hair. This prevents the hair from drying out and gives it a nice shine at the same time.

GELS
The use of gels is to help lock in and define curl patterns. Gels can be used after applying moisturizer or with your oil. There are various types of gels some offer built in conditioner which fights frizz; others offer proteins and other nutrients to help the hair.

Tip: *Use gel sparingly until you are comfortable with the hard or softness of the gel on your hair. I use gels less than 10% of the time, makes my hair too stiff.*

STEP SIX:

REFRESHING SPRAY
Natural curls dries out quickly, and a refreshing spritz will help to put the moisture back in. Hair is also easier to style when wet or moisturized, which will eliminate excessive breakage. I use this DIY spritz daily.

DIY Refreshing Spritz

- One 16 oz. plastic bottle
- Pour 8 oz. of Aloe Vera Juice

- Fill the other half with distilled water (or boil water)
- Apply 2-3 drops of your favorite essential oil, shake and use spritz to wake up your curls.

I became a 'product junkie' early in the process because I didn't know what I was doing or what would work best for my hair. I ruled out a lot of products and now my die-hards and <u>recommendations are</u>: See list at: www.sisthanatural.com

Hair Care Routine

There are several steps to my hair care routine; morning, bed-time, weekly and monthly. Daily steps are shorter then washday, which is a semi-long process. Sometimes while I'm deep conditioning on washday I would put a plastic cap on and wrap my head with a beautiful scarf and go shopping, to the gym or do whatever I have to for that week-end. The heat from my wrapped head does a great job of activating the conditioner onto my hair.

Morning:

- Refreshing Spritz
- Leave in moisturizer
- Oil sealant
- Style

Bed Time Protection:

Just spritz, moisturize, seal and protect. Depending on the length, place hair in a loose high bun before putting your scarf on. For a more stretched look; part hair in two and do a two-strand twist, pinning twist in opposite direction around your head. Wrap with a silk scarf to keep moisture in and protect the hair. (Sleeping on a satin pillowcase will also protect your hair from breakage.) In the morning, undo & style.

Tip: *After doing the bedtime regime, place a plastic cap and then a scarf over your hair, this will give extra moisture & less work in the morning, just style.*

Wash Day

- Pre wash
- Co-wash
- Finger detangle in shower
- Deep condition under dryer for 20 minutes
- Rinse out
- Towel dry excess water
- Apply water base leave-in moisturizer
- Seal with oil
- Air dry then style (or just wash & go)

Weekly

- Wash hair once a week & with shorter hair twice a week until hair starts growing out. (Water is good for the hair so use it.)

Bi-Monthly

- Deep Condition twice a month
- Hot oil treatment twice a month

These are some of the basic steps to start you on your hair journey until you get into your own routine. Before long you'll be experimenting with your own DIY masks, oils, shampoos and conditioners. Have fun with it!

Protective Styles

The best description of protective styling is putting your hair into a style where you tuck your ends away from the atmosphere to protect them from damage while your hair grows out.

Here are a few of the many protective styles that are available. You will be able to find a more detailed list of styles and how to create them on the Internet.

- Bantu Knots- (Jamaican term-'coolie bump')-section and twirl hair into small individual bumps.
- High-top bun with ends tucked under

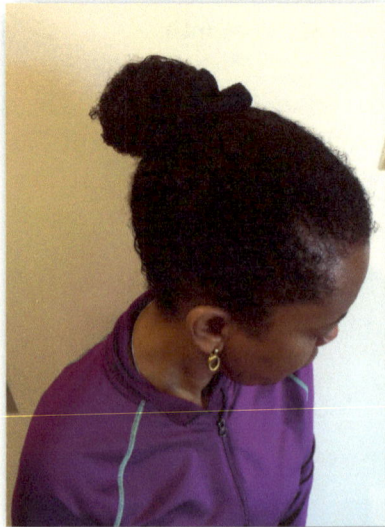

- Braid- part hair in several sections and three-strands twist each section.
- Up-do Example

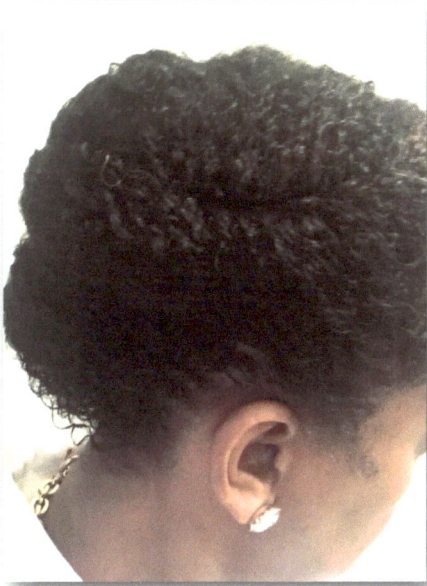

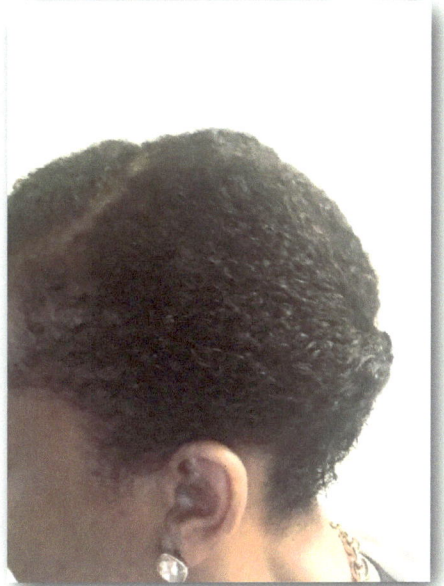

- Two-strands twists- Part in sections and twist, then pin up or let hang.
- Wigs – I have not used but it's an option.

Hair Growth Tips

Now that you have decided to go natural, a change in your lifestyle will also help. Here are some additional tips to help with your hair growth journey. I have used all of these at some point during my journey.

1. **Biotin and the complex B Vitamins**: Are components needed to grow hair; it increases circulation to the scalp, which encourages hair growth.
2. **Moisture**: Hair will grow with less breakage when moisture is added to the shaft. Moisture comes from conditioning or adding plain old Co2/DIY spritz.
3. **Protein**: Hair is made of protein & insufficient amounts can discourage hair growth. You can add protein to your diet by adding whey protein powder to your favorite smoothie or you can eat meat or dairy to get the necessary amounts. (If you are a vegan, then use the protein powder)
4. **Stimulating Scalp**: I found this head massager at a cosmetic store. It feels Sooo good on the head! It helps to increase circulation, which will encourage hair growth. (Psss! You can also use your fingers)

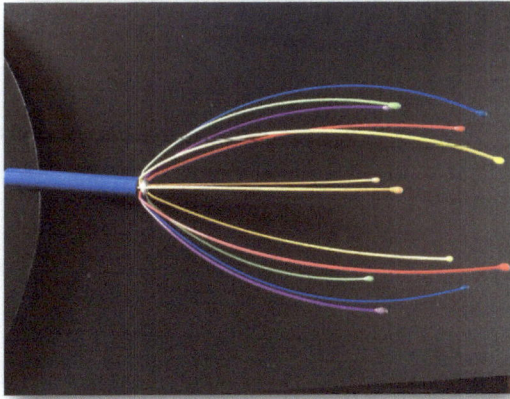

5. **Trim Ends**: My take on this is to only do it if you have split ends.
6. **Vitamin C**: Is also a needed component for healthy hair.
7. **Vitamin E**: Is another component, which will stimulate the circulation in the scalp while encouraging hair growth.
8. **Water**: Drinking water is beneficial to the overall well being of the body, and when the body is hydrated it also encourages hair growth. Drink a minimum of 4 to 8 cups a day.
9. **Cost:** Have you ever gone to the beauty shop to get a perm, color, press N curl, braids or weave? Guess what? It cost less to go natural. Just don't become a product junkie. Once you've settled into the products that work best for your hair type, you will see the savings.
10. **Thinning hair**: The following oils will penetrate the shaft and get deep into the follicle of the hair stimulating hair growth. (1) Avocado Oil (2) Olive Oil (3) Coconut Oil (4) Castor Oil. Massage high quality oil onto the thinning area daily to see great results.
11. **You are what you eat**: Making some lifestyle changes will help with the growth process. Healthier diet should include more vegetables, fruits and less sugar, which are highly beneficial for overall health and hair growth.

12. **Problem scalp:** What about dandruff and other scalp irritations? Use one of the following or a combination to fight the 'flakes:'

    - Apple cider vinegar rinse. (See pg. 6)
    - Tea Tree oil is an effective remedy, which has antibacterial and antifungal properties.
    - Rosemary or Basil oil (or both) Add to warm distilled water and use as a rinse.

13. **Above all, be patient!** "Rome wasn't built in a day" The myth that black hair can't grow long has been shattered! Check out all the testimonials on YouTube under natural black hair. "Yes it can! No matter what the hair type, but you must be patient and do the work to get it there."

    "Check out my testimony on the next page"

Hair Growth Journey

" A Picture is worth a thousand words"

Pre-Big Chop April 2013

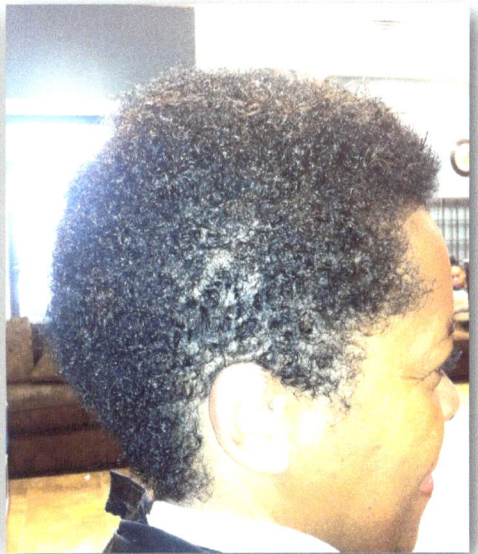

Big Chop (BC) May 2013

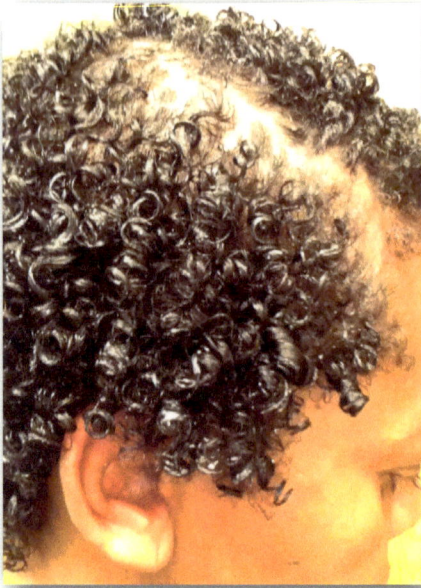

May 2014 – 1 yr. BC

Dec 2014 – 1 ½ yr.

May 2015 2 yrs. BC

Dec 2015 2 ½ yrs. BC

Benefits of Oil

SSENTIAL OILS are concentrated aromatic essences of plants. They get extracted from various plants, wood and fruits. The following list of essential and carrier oils are only a fraction of what is available. Here are some of the main ones I use.

Tip: *Always dilute essential oils, preferable with carrier oil before using on hair or skin.*

Carrot Seed:

- Benefits: Replenishes, nourishes, and restores the skin. It also helps to smooth and improve the tone of aging skin.

Geranium Oil:

- Benefits: Has great fragrances, provides the skin with toning, and cleansing properties. It also has antioxidants.

Jasmine Oil:

- Benefits: Improves skin elasticity. Can also be used to fade stretch marks & acne scars.

Lavender Oil:

- Benefits: Provides relief from various skin problems, and very calming for itchy skin. Helps the body to relax and distress.

Neroli Oil:

- Benefits: Increase elasticity of mature skin, also great for wrinkles & sagging skin.

Rosemary Oil:

- Benefits: Has a strong fragrance; also has antiseptic and antibacterial for problem skin. Will help to stimulate blood circulation in the body. Can be used as a daily rinse to retain hair color & is most effective on dark hair.

Ylang Ylang Oil:

- Benefits: Smooth fine lines and improves skin elasticity. Also helps to promote hair growth and thickness.

CARRIER **OILS** also known as base/vegetable oil is used to dilute essential oil and absolutes before they are applied to the skin or hair.

Tip: *Keep all oils in a cool dark place to prolong the life of the oil, and keep it fresh.*

Almond Oil:

- Benefits: Great for itchy inflamed skin, very moisturizing and high in fatty acid. Can be used as a moisturizer by itself.

Apricot Kernel Oil:

- Benefits: Works as a light moisturizer, penetrating deep into the skin. Also acts as a cleanser.

Avocado Oil:

- Benefits: A deep penetrating moisturizer rich with fatty acids as well as vitamins. Often used for creams, lotions, and on hair & skin.

Argan Oil:

- Benefits: Moisturizes and condition both hair and skin. It is filled with fatty acids as well as vitamin E.

Basil:

- Benefits: Known to stimulate hair growth is antibacterial which helps with the scalp and other irritations.

Coconut Oil:

- Benefits: Softens and moisturizes both the hair and skin. Used in creams and lotions to penetrate both.

Castor Oil:

- Benefits: Has antifungal, antibacterial properties, which benefits the hair and skin.

Emu Oil:

- Benefits: Has anti-inflammatory, antibacterial and moisturizing properties. Also great for scars and stretch marks.

Evening Primrose Oil:

- Benefits: Great for reducing acne, breakouts and smoothing skin. Used as a moisturizer for the skin.

Frankincense:

- Benefits: Has anti-inflammatory and antibacterial properties. Helps to heal the skin, great for blemish, and sagging skin. Also used with other carrier oils for moisture to the skin.

Jojoba Oil:

- Benefits: Great moisturizer for the hair, skin and nails.

Myrrh Oil:

- Benefits: Great for aging skin, provides anti-inflammatory properties that help to improve skin tone, firmness and appearance of fine lines and wrinkles.

Olive Oil:

- Benefits: Helps to moisturize the skin and the hair. Also great for stretch marks and has many vitamins and minerals.

Rose Hip Oil:

- Benefits: Provides healing and rejuvenating properties along with fatty acids and anti-aging qualities for damage skin.

Safflower Oil:

- Benefits: Has many fatty acids, vitamins A, D and E. Great moisturizer and penetrates well into the skin.

Tea Tree Oil:

- Benefits: Has numerous properties, which includes antibacterial, antiviral and antiseptic. Can be use on fungus, acne, and many other skin related issues.

Skin Care Tips

OIL MOISTURISER

Using natural oils helps to lock in moisture and protect the skin from the harsh elements. Many natural oils have nutrients and other anti-aging properties, which are naturally great for healing and repairing the skin. Natural oils will not clog pores and is easily absorbed into the skin. (I got rid of my lotions and creams when my skin and face became sensitive and started breaking out two years ago) I love how soft the oil makes my skin feels. After getting out of the shower or washing your face do not dry off. While the skin is still moist, apply your DIY oil mixture onto your skin or face.

BODY MOISTURIZING DIY

- 8 oz. plastic/glass bottle
- 1 oz. Avocado oil
- 1 tbsp. Carrot oil
- 1 oz. Castor oil
- 2-1/2 oz. Olive oil
- 2-1/2 oz. Jojoba oil
- 3 tbsp. Sweet Almond oil
- 8 drops Geranium oil

- 6 drops Lavender oil
- (To make a larger mixture, double or triple the ingredients)

DAILY FACE MOISTURIZER

- Small glass bottle
- 5 drops Avocado oil
- 2 drops Evening Primrose oil
- 1 drop Geranium oil
- 15 drops Jojoba oil
- 2 drops Lavender oil
- ¾ oz. Sweet Almond oil
- 1 drop Ylan Ylang oil
- (Double or triple the ingredients to make a larger batch)

NIGHT MOISTURIZER

- 5-10 drops Almond oil
- 6 tbsp. Aloe Vera Gel *
- 1 ½ tbsp. Coconut oil (lbs.)
- 1 tsp. Vitamin E oil
- 5 drops Frankincense
- 5 drops Lavender oil
- 1 tsp. Olive oil
- 1 tbsp. Raw Shea Butter *

Pour ingredients in ceramics bowl and blend well. Pour into a 4 oz. glass jar. (The Shea Butter will be grainy, so blend well. * May be optional)

Tip: *Using organics oils will give you the most benefits. Always perform a skin test before using oils to rule out any allergies.*

NOTES

1. Additional information on blending oils can be found in Young Living Essential Oils at www.youngliving.com

2. Essential Oil benefits reference from 'The healing intelligence of essential oils'

3. **Have fun on your hair journey!**

www.ingramcontent.com/pod-product-compliance
Lightning Source LLC
Chambersburg PA
CBHW041803040426
42448CB00001B/27